T0380958

Who Am I?

Melissa Gole

To order additional copies of this book, contact:
Xlibris
1-800-455-039
www.xlibris.com.au
Orders@Xlibris.com.au

Dedicated to those caring for and loving people living with dementia.

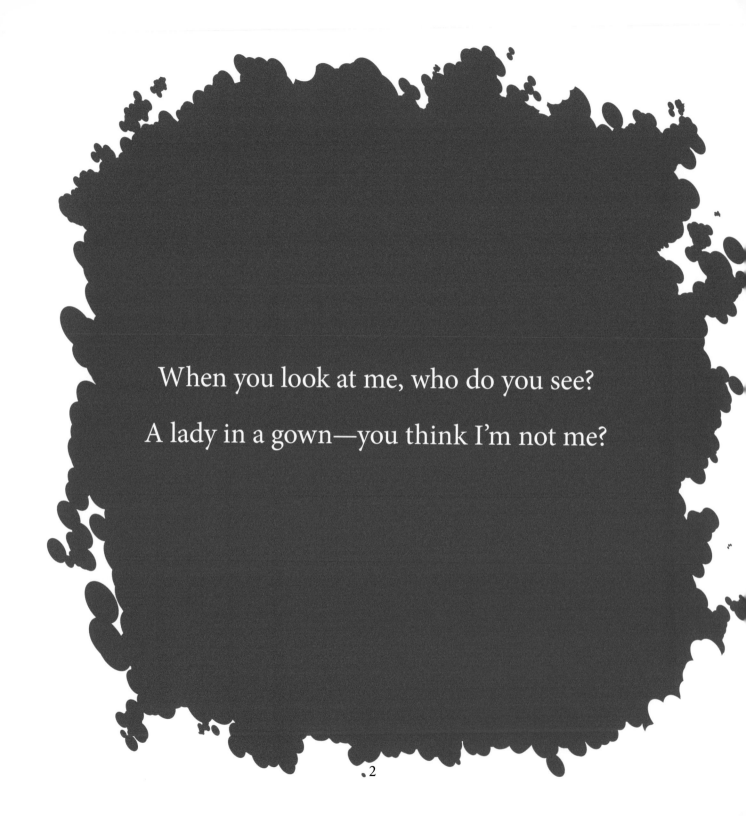

When you look at me, who do you see?

A lady in a gown—you think I'm not me?

I am the mother who loved you
and held you in my arms.

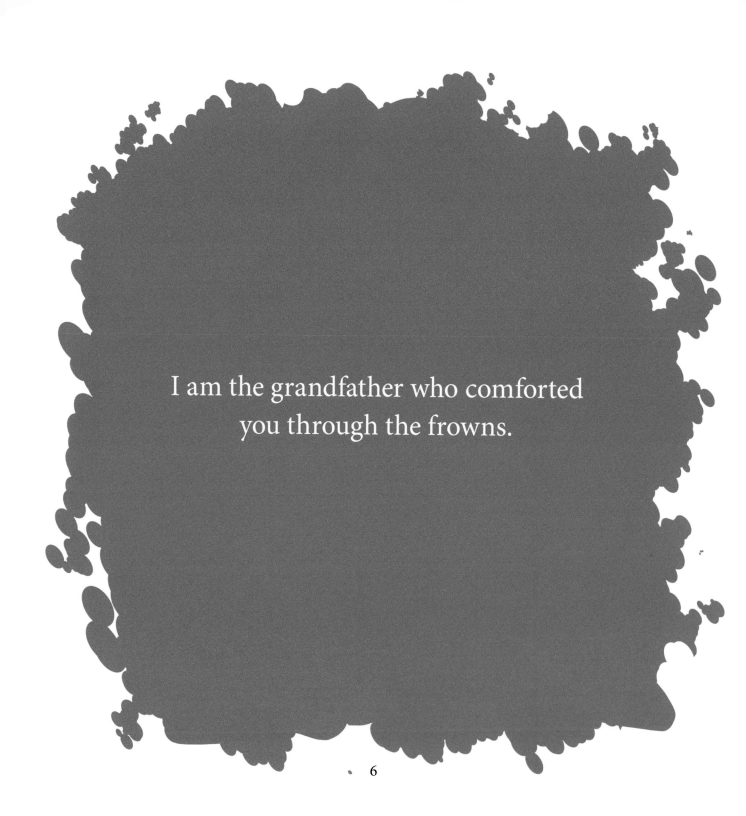

I am the grandfather who comforted
you through the frowns.

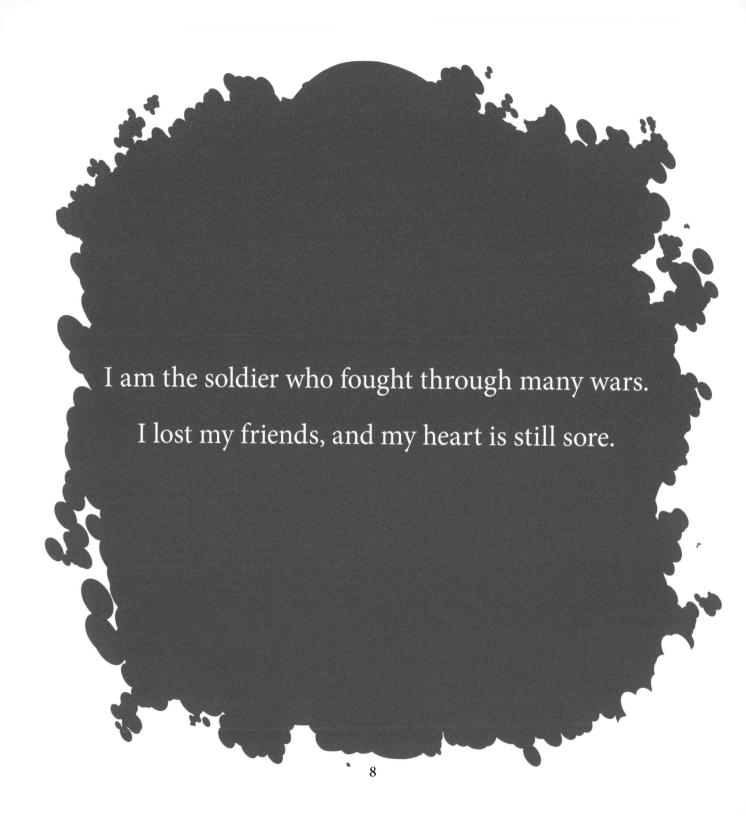

I am the soldier who fought through many wars.

I lost my friends, and my heart is still sore.

I am the policeman who worked a very tough beat.

I didn't know who I might bump into in the street.

I have a big family and they all wore Blue.

We were all there to serve and protect you.

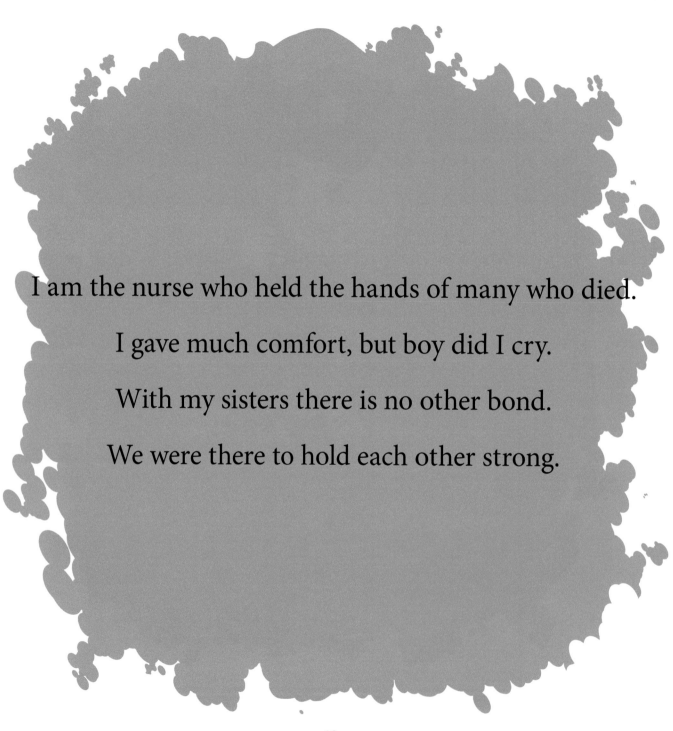

I am the nurse who held the hands of many who died.

I gave much comfort, but boy did I cry.

With my sisters there is no other bond.

We were there to hold each other strong.

I am the cleaner who woke up at four in the morn.

I'm ready for work now, and it's not even dawn.

I am the Holocaust survivor. I am iron strong.

What I went through was so very wrong.

When I shower it brings back the fear.

I see your uniform and think the animals are near.

Though I might look scary, I'm very afraid.

I need you to tell me we'll be OK.

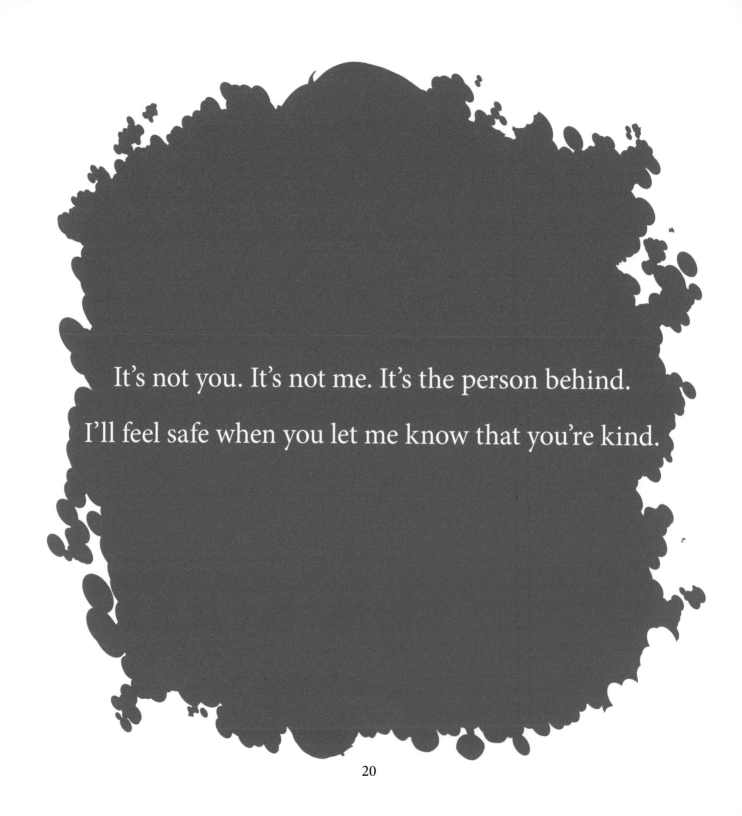

It's not you. It's not me. It's the person behind.

I'll feel safe when you let me know that you're kind.

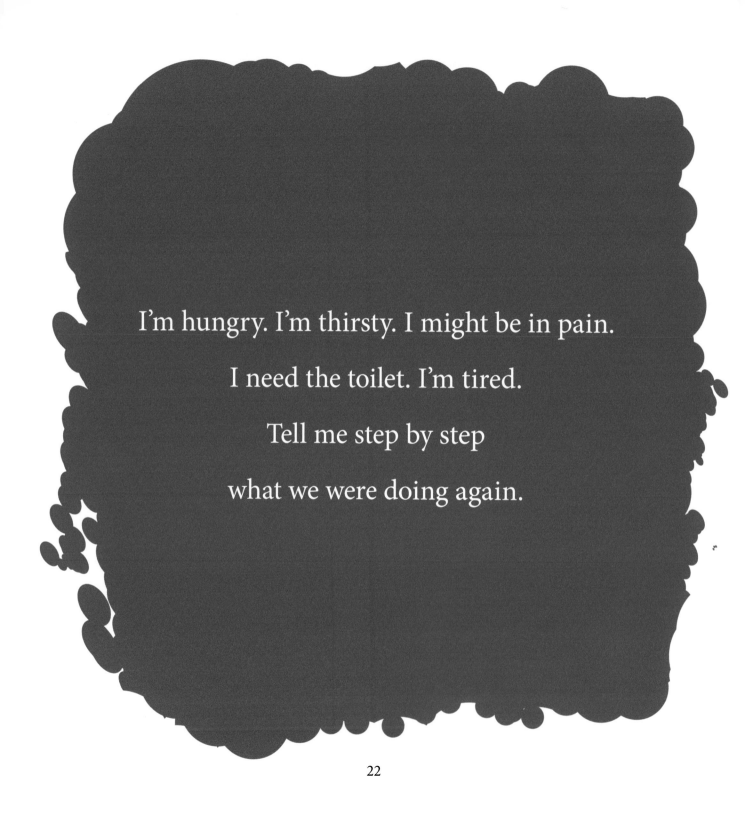

I'm hungry. I'm thirsty. I might be in pain.

I need the toilet. I'm tired.

Tell me step by step

what we were doing again.

I am still here. I'm the person you knew.

You're my safe face, my home. And I'll always love you.

Let's take time to remember our pictures and food,
remember our music and the things we'd do.

For now I am here,

so let's make memories to cherish.

You are my love, and the one I hold dear.

Australian Resources

Alzheimers Australia
www.alz.org

Commonwealth Carer Respite Centre (24 hours)
1-800-059-059

Dementia Australia
www.dementia.org.au
1-800-100-500

Dementia Behaviour Management Advisory Service (DBMAS)
1-800-699-799

My Aged Care
www.myagedcare.gov.au
1-800-200-422

Printed in the United States
By Bookmasters